REGIONAL
WILD AMERICA

UNIQUE ANIMALS OF THE
SOUTHWEST

By Tanya Lee Stone

BLACKBIRCH PRESS

An imprint of Thomson Gale, a part of The Thomson Corporation

THOMSON

GALE

Detroit • New York • San Francisco • San Diego • New Haven, Conn. • Waterville, Maine • London • Munich

THOMSON

GALE

For more information, contact
Blackbirch Press
27500 Drake Rd.
Farmington Hills, MI 48331-3535
Or you can visit our Internet site at http://www.gale.com

Photo Credits: Cover image: © Corel Corporation; Tom Boyden/Lonely Planet Images, 10; © CORBIS, 16; © Corel Corporation, 4 (inset), 5, 6, 7, 11, 13 (top), 18, 19, 22 (bottom); © Michael & Patricia Fogden/CORBIS, 20; Heidi & Hans-Juergen Koch/Minden Pictures, 8; © Joe McDonald/CORBIS, 21; Yva Momatuik/John Eastcott/Minden Pictures, 14; © David A. Northcott/CORBIS, 15; Pete Oxford/Minden Pictures, 9; Photos.com, 12, 13 (bottom), 22 (top), 23; © Galen Rowell/CORBIS, 17; Steve Zmina, 4 (map)

LIBRARY OF CONGRESS CATALOGING-IN-PUBLICATION DATA

Stone, Tanya Lee.
   Unique animals of the Southwest / by Tanya Lee Stone.
      p. cm. — (Regional wild America)
Summary: Describes various animals of the southwest region of the United States.
   Includes bibliographical references and index.
   ISBN 1-56711-970-0 (hard cover : alk. paper)
   1. Animals—Southwestern States—Juvenile literature. I. Title II. Series: Stone, Tanya Lee. Regional wild America.
   QL157.S69S76 2005
   591.976—dc22
                                                                          2004011180

Printed in the United States of America
10 9 8 7 6 5 4 3 2 1

Contents

Introduction 5
Racing Around! 6
Armored Armadillos 8
Prickly Pear Peccaries 10
Cunning Coyotes 12
Raccoon Relatives 14
Desert Diggers 16
Leapin' Lizards! 18
Serious Snakes! 20
Creepy Crawlies 22
Glossary 24
For More Information 24
Index 24

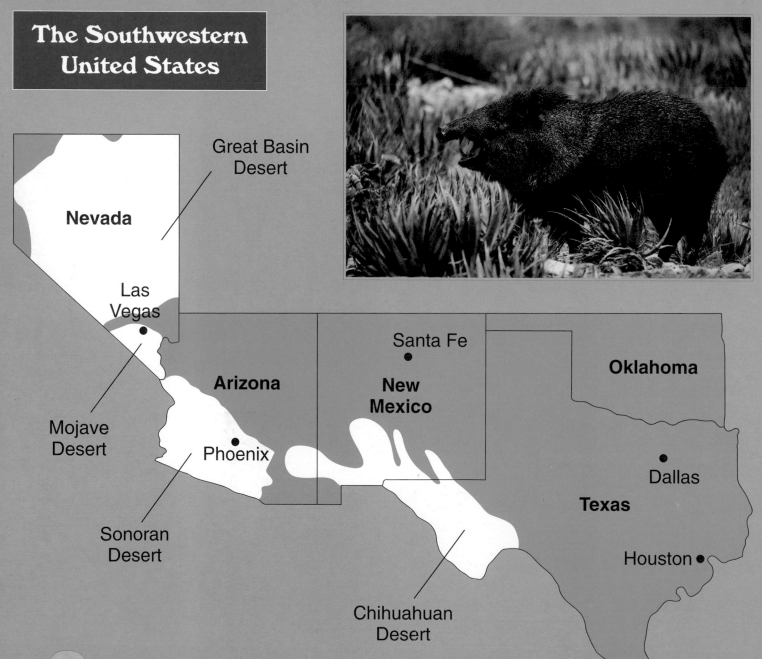

The Southwestern United States

Great Basin Desert

Nevada

Las Vegas

Mojave Desert

Arizona

Phoenix

Sonoran Desert

Santa Fe

New Mexico

Oklahoma

Dallas

Texas

Houston

Chihuahuan Desert

There are four major deserts in the Southwest region. Parts of the Chihuahuan Desert fall in Texas and New Mexico. The Sonoran Desert covers almost half of Arizona. Part of the Mojave Desert crosses into Nevada. And the Great Basin Desert blankets a huge part of Nevada.

A variety of wildlife lives in these deserts, and in the rest of the Southwest region. Some of these animals are especially well known.

A variety of unique animals, including the Gila monster (above) and the peccary (opposite), make their home in the American Southwest.

Roadrunners use their long legs to chase down prey. Here, a roadrunner carries a lizard off for an afternoon meal.

Racing Around!

The roadrunner is a common sight in the Southwest and is the state bird of New Mexico. These birds are made for running! They have long legs that are very strong. Their feet are strong, too. Roadrunners can run more than 15 miles (24km) per hour! They have long tails that help them balance when they run. Although these birds can fly, they do not do it very often.

Roadrunners use their speed to escape predators (an animal that hunts another animal for food). Hawks and coyotes are their main predators. Roadrunners also run to chase prey (an animal that is hunted by another animal for food). These birds eat insects, lizards, and snakes. They also eat bird eggs and small rodents.

In addition to being fast runners, roadrunners are able to hop around and change direction quickly. This helps confuse or tire another animal. Roadrunners use this trick on rattlesnakes. As soon as the snake gets tired from trying to strike at the roadrunner, the bird stabs the snake with its strong beak. Roadrunners are so fast on their feet they can even snatch a hummingbird or dragonfly that flies too close!

A roadrunner stops to check its surroundings. Roadrunners are fast on their feet and can change direction quickly.

Armored Armadillos

Armadillos are related to sloths and anteaters. The nine-banded armadillo is the state mammal of Texas. It is also found in Oklahoma and in southern states east of Texas. Armadillos are mainly nocturnal. This means they sleep during the day and are active at night. They sometimes search for food in the daytime. They eat ants, beetles, and termites. Their sharp sense of smell helps them find food. They use their long, sticky tongues to pull ants and termites from their nests. Armadillos eat other kinds of insects, too. They also feed on fruit, bird eggs, snakes, and carrion (dead animals).

This armadillo uses its sharp sense of smell to find ants, beetles, and termites (below). Armadillos curl into a ball to protect their soft belly when they sense danger (opposite).

An armadillo is about 18 to 22 inches (46 to 56cm) long. Its tail adds an extra 9 to 15 inches (23 to 38cm). It has a long, pointy nose and large, pointy ears. Armadillos are born with soft, leathery skin. As they grow, their skin starts to harden. They develop bony plates that cover most of their bodies.

This bony plating is used for protection. When it is in danger, an armadillo can curl up. That way, its soft belly stays safe. This protects it from enemies. Armadillos also use speed to escape enemies. They slip into burrows to hide when necessary. Armadillos use their strong legs and claws to dig burrows more than 6 feet (2m) deep and 15 feet (5m) long. Burrows are used for sleeping, escaping danger, and nesting. Nine-banded armadillos are the only mammals that give birth to four identical babies.

Prickly Pear Peccaries

Collared peccaries are a common sight throughout the Southwest. This mammal looks like a pig, but belongs to its own family. They are 35 to 45 inches (89 to 114cm) long. They weigh 30 to 60 pounds (14 to 27kg). A collared peccary gets its name from the band of fur around its neck. It is also called a javelina or a musk hog.

Smell plays a big part in this animal's life. It gives off a strong odor and can be smelled from a few hundred feet away. It is also good at using its nose to find other members of its herd. These animals usually live in groups of twelve to fifteen. They have a scent gland on their backs. This is used to mark territory.

Baby peccaries can keep up with their mothers a day after their birth.

Collared peccaries also use their excellent sense of smell to find food. They can sniff out roots several inches under the ground. They eat roots, herbs, nuts, berries, and grasses. They also feed on fruit and worms. One of their favorite foods is the prickly pear cactus.

Females usually give birth to two babies. The whole herd helps look out for the young. A baby can travel with the herd when it is only a day old. These animals can run fast—up to 25 miles (40km) per hour! They usually choose to run from a predator. They also make noises to alert the rest of the herd. If it has to, a collared peccary will use its sharp teeth on an enemy. A collared peccary can even fight off a bobcat or coyote.

A collard peccary uses its excellent sense of smell to sniff out its favorite foods.

Cunning Coyotes

A coyote is a medium-sized member of the dog family. It is related to the wolf, but is much smaller. It has pointy ears and a droopy, bushy tail. Its tail is about as long as its body. Coyotes can be found in most parts of North America. But these wild dogs are a common sight in the Southwest. They even live in neighborhoods and cities.

Like all wild dogs, coyotes communicate with each other through sounds. Coyotes howl, bark, whine, and growl. In fact, scientists have discovered that coyotes make many different sounds. Different sounds have different meanings, such as "danger" or "keep out!" Coyotes also communicate with each other by moving their ears and tails in certain ways.

A coyote howls for its pack. Coyotes howl, whine, and growl to communicate with each other.

These coyotes hunt together for their favorite foods but will eat almost anything. Below, a coyote feasts on a bird.

Coyotes hunt alone, in pairs, or in a small group. They have keen hearing and an excellent sense of smell. A coyote can run up to 40 miles (64km) per hour. They are great swimmers and can leap up to 13 feet (4m). All of these things make coyotes good hunters. They will eat almost anything, but seem to prefer small mammals such as mice, rats, rabbits, and squirrels. They also eat carrion, fruits, and vegetables.

Coyotes often mate for life. The female usually gives birth to her pups inside a safe, cozy den. Coyotes either build their own dens or take over the home of another animal. A coyote pair raises its young together. Pups are born blind, and with floppy ears. Within about ten days, their ears start to stand up and they are able to see.

Raccoon Relatives

Ringtails and coatis are both related to raccoons, and both live in the Southwest. The ringtail is Arizona's state mammal. It is also found in Nevada, Oklahoma, Texas, and New Mexico. A ringtail is about the size of a house cat. It gets its name from its long, bushy tail that has black and white rings.

The ringtail (above) hunts at night, while the coati (opposite) looks for food during the day. Both are excellent climbers.

Ringtails are nocturnal. They sleep most of the day in small spaces such as rock crevices and hollow logs. At night, they hunt. They are expert climbers and have excellent hearing and eyesight. This makes them good hunters. Ringtails eat small mammals, lizards, frogs, and birds. They also eat snakes, insects, and fruit.

White-nosed coatis also eat both plants and animals. They like fruits, nuts, insects, and eggs. They also eat rodents, lizards, and snakes. Coatis eat carrion, too.

As its name suggests, the white-nosed coati has a white snout. Unlike ringtails, this coati is a diurnal animal. This means it sleeps at night and is active during the day. Like ringtails, white-nosed coatis are good climbers. Their long tails help them balance while in trees.

Desert Diggers

A tortoise is a type of turtle that lives on land. The desert tortoise is the state reptile of Nevada. It is a threatened species. That means it is against the law to harm them. Desert tortoises can live up to 80 years if left alone! Reptiles such as the tortoise are cold-blooded animals. This means that the temperature of their bodies changes with the temperature of the air around them.

Desert tortoises are cold-blooded animals that can live to eighty years old.

Desert tortoises live in both the Sonoran and Mojave deserts. They are able to live in areas where temperatures on the ground reach 140 degrees Fahrenheit (60°C)! Desert tortoises live in underground burrows to escape the heat. Sometimes, they look for shade under big rocks. Their burrows also protect them from the cold temperatures in the winter. In fact, desert tortoises spend most of their lives in their burrows.

Tortoises are plant eaters. Here, a tortoise nibbles on grasses in its path.

Desert tortoises weigh about 8 to 15 pounds (4 to 7kg). Their carapace (top shell) is 9 to 15 inches (23 to 38cm) long. These tortoises have strong front limbs for digging. They use them to dig burrows. Desert tortoises also dig shallow basins to catch rainwater. They remember where the basins are and return to them when it rains. These tortoises are plant eaters. They get some of the water they need from the grasses and wildflowers they eat. If necessary, a desert tortoise can live a year without water.

A collard lizard eats its prey. Collard lizards hunt mostly in the cooler morning and late afternoon hours.

Leapin' Lizards!

The Southwest is home to many kinds of lizards. The collared lizard is Oklahoma's state reptile. It is also found in the other states of this region. Other common lizards throughout the Southwest include the chuckwalla and the Gila monster.

Collared lizards are diurnal, but are mostly active in the morning or late afternoon when it is not as hot. They are swift runners. They sometimes stand upright on their back legs when they run. Males often sit on high rocks where they have a good view of the area. This may be to guard their territory, watch for females, or spot prey. Collared lizards mostly eat insects and other small lizards.

Chuckwallas are herbivores. A chuckwalla likes flowers, leaves, and buds. Chuckwallas have a unique way of protecting themselves from predators. They have folds of loose skin on their flat bodies. To escape danger, a chuckwalla will crawl into a small space such as a crack in a ledge. It then gulps air and puffs up its body so it becomes wedged into place. It is practically impossible to get a chuckwalla out until it is good and ready to come out!

A Gila monster does not need much protection. It is one of only two venomous lizards in the world. It is a beaded lizard. Its rounded scales look a bit like beads. Gila monsters are big and colorful. They have strong claws made for digging. These reptiles spend hot desert days under rocks or in holes they dig. They come out at dusk to hunt. Gila monsters move slowly, except when striking prey. A Gila monster will clamp its jaws onto a small mammal or bird quickly. Its venom then flows into the animal's wound and kills it.

Because their colorful rounded scales resemble beads, Gila monsters like this one are called beaded lizards.

Snakes are reptiles. They are cold-blooded animals. When they need to cool their bodies down, they look for shade. When they need to warm up, they bask in the sun. Many different kinds of snakes live in the Southwest. Some are poisonous and some are not.

Coral snakes and rattlesnakes are particularly dangerous. Coral snakes are very colorful. They have red, yellow, and black bands. Other snakes with similar colors are not poisonous, so it is important to be able to tell them apart. One easy way is to remember the saying, "red touches yellow—deadly fellow." This refers to the coral snake. Their coloring warns off predators. Coral snakes use their venom to kill prey. They mainly eat lizards and other kinds of snakes.

A coral snake uses its powerful venom to kill another snake.

This rattlesnake has just shed its skin, adding a new piece to its rattle.

There are many different kinds of rattlesnakes, but they all have jointed rattles at the ends of their tails. Each time a rattlesnake molts (sheds its skin) a new piece of the rattle is formed. Rattlesnakes shake their rattles when they are threatened.

A rattlesnake is a pit viper. This kind of snake has two large pits in its head. The pits are heat-sensing organs. This helps a rattlesnake find its prey. Rattlesnakes also pick up nearby scents with their flickering tongues. A rattlesnake will strike its victim and inject the animal with its venom. Rattlesnakes eat small mammals, lizards, and even birds. A western diamondback can swallow an animal that outweighs it!

Creepy Crawlies

Scorpions are found on every continent except Antarctica. They are well suited to the desert and are common in the Southwest. Several different kinds of scorpions live in this region. Scorpions are arachnids and have four pairs of legs. They also have two pincer claws.

A mother scorpion carries her babies on her back (above). This scorpion (below) used the poisonous stinger on its tail to kill a beetle for its lunch.

A scorpion has a sharp stinger on the end of its tail. This stinger packs a punch—it comes with poison glands! A scorpion warns off predators with its poisonous stinger. It also uses the venom to kill its prey. Scorpions eat spiders, insects, and other scorpions! A scorpion attacks by swinging its tail up over its body and plunging its stinger into the prey. The most poisonous scorpion in the United States—the bark scorpion—makes its home in Arizona. It is quite dangerous to humans.

Tarantulas live in many parts of the Southwest. They are arachnids, too. Their eight legs are hairy! Although they have eight eyes, they still cannot see very well. Tarantulas are the largest spiders in the world. Their bodies are 1 to 3 inches (2.54 to 8cm) long. Tarantulas are generally not poisonous to people. But these spiders have poison glands inside their jaws. The glands are connected to two pointed fangs. When it senses an insect nearby, a tarantula runs quickly to it and stabs it with its fangs. The poison kills the insect and the spider can begin its meal.

The largest spiders in the world, tarantulas have two pointed fangs in addition to their eight hairy legs.

There are many unique and wonderful animals that live in the Southwest region. They all add to the area's richness and beauty.

Glossary

Carapace The top of a turtle's shell.
Carnivore An animal that mainly eats meat.
Diurnal Asleep at night and active during the day.
Herbivore An animal that mainly eats plants.
Nocturnal Asleep during the day and active at night.

Omnivore An animal that eats plants and other animals.
Predator An animal that hunts another animal for food.
Prey An animal that is hunted by another animal.

For More Information

Arnosky, Jim. *Watching Desert Wildlife*. Washington, D.C.: National Geographic, 1998.

Jacobs, Lee. *Turtles*. San Diego, CA: Blackbirch Press, 2003.

Ricciuti, Edward. *What on Earth is a Chuckwalla?* San Diego, CA: Blackbirch Press, 1994.

Swinburne, Stephen R. *Coyote: North America's Dog*. Honesdale, PA: Boyds Mills Press, 1999.

Index

arachnids, 22–23
Arizona state mammal, 14–15
armadillos, 8–9

chuckwallas, 19
coatis, 14, 15
collared lizards, 18
collared peccaries, 10–11
coral snakes, 20

coyotes, 12–13

deserts, 5

Gila monsters, 19

javelinas, 10–11

lizards, 18–19

musk hogs, 10–11

New Mexico state bird, 6–7
nine-banded armadillos, 8
nocturnal animals, 8–9, 14–15

Oklahoma state reptile, 18

pit vipers, 21

rattlesnakes, 20, 21
reptiles, 17, 20
ringtails, 14–15
roadrunners, 6–7

scorpions, 22–23
snakes, 20–21

tarantulas, 23
Texas state mammal, 8–9
tortoises, 16–17